The ABC'S of

LGBT+

Guided Journal

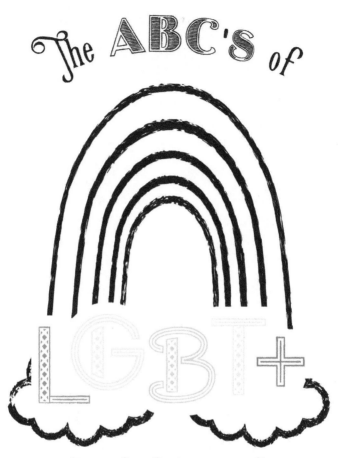

# The ABC's of LGBT+

## Guided Journal

A Companion Guide to Ash Hardell's
*The ABC's of LGBT*

## Ash Hardell

**mango**
PUBLISHING GROUP
CORAL GABLES

Cover Design: Megan Werner
Illustrations: August Osterloh
Layout & Design: Megan Werner

For permission requests, please contact the publisher at:
Mango Publishing Group
2850 S Douglas Road, 4th Floor
Coral Gables, FL 33134 USA
info@mango.bz

For special orders, quantity sales, course adoptions and corporate
sales, please email the publisher at sales@mango.bz. For trade
and wholesale sales, please contact Ingram Publisher Services at
customer.service@ingramcontent.com or +1.800.509.4887.

The ABCs of LGBT+ Guided Journal: A Companion Guide to Ash
Hardell's *The ABCs of LGBT+*

ISBN: (p) 978-1-64250-947-2
BISAC category code: SEL045000, SELF-HELP / Journaling

Printed in the United States of America

# Introduction

What is this journal for? Both the original book (*The ABCs of LGBT+*) and this journal aim to help guide you on your journey as you learn about and navigate the many identities within the vast and dynamic spectrum of sexuality. Your exploration of this topic will undoubtably leave you with both questions and new ideas. So we hope that this journal, with its informative artwork, definitions, and writing prompts, will help you work through how you're feeling and what you're learning. Use this journal to help you process what this journey means for you, your family and friends, and your future.

# Words to Be Familiar With

**Abrosexual/romantic:** Someone who experiences a fluid and/or changing orientation.

**Ace:** An umbrella term for any identity on the asexual spectrum. Also shorthand for "asexual."

**Ace/aroflux:** Someone who experiences varying degrees of attraction.

**Affirm:** to support, validate, and/or assert that something is true/correct.

**Agender/genderless:** Someone who is without gender, gender neutral, and/or rejects the concept of gender for themselves.

**Ally:** Someone who does not identify as LGBTQIA+, but actively supports the community.

**Androgyne:**  A non-binary gender in which a person is *both* a man and woman, *neither* a man nor woman, and/or *somewhere in between* man and woman.

**Androgynesexual/romantic:** Someone who is attracted to androgyny.

**Androgynous:** Possessing qualities which are traditionally associated as *both* masculine and feminine, *neither* masculine nor feminine, and/or *in between* masculine and feminine.

**Aporagender:** Both a specific gender identity and an umbrella term for being a non-binary gender separate from man, woman, and anything in between while still having a very strong and specific gendered feeling.

**Appropriation:** Borrowing or adopting something as one's own when it did not originate from them or their culture. This type of use occurs without proper understanding, credit, and/or permission. *(Example: white people wearing feathered headdresses as costumes during Halloween.)*

**Aro:** An umbrella term for any identity on the aromantic spectrum. Also shorthand for "aromantic."

**Aromantic:** An umbrella term, or stand-alone identifier, for someone who experiences little or no romantic attraction.

**Asexual:** An umbrella term, or stand-alone identifier, for someone who experiences little or no sexual attraction.

**Autosexual/romantic:** Being able to elicit a sexual/romantic attraction from yourself by yourself and/or not desiring to partake in sexual activity with others, but still enjoying being sexually intimate with yourself.

**Bicurious:** Someone curious about having sexual/romantic attractions and/or experiences with more than one gender.

**Bigender:** Someone who has/experiences two genders.

**Binary:** The rigid way society divides sex and gender into only two categories: 1) male/men and 2) female/women.

**Bisexual/romantic:** Being attracted to two or more genders.

**CAFAB/CAMAB:** These are acronyms for "coercively assigned female at birth" and "coercively assigned male at birth."

**Cisgender/Cis:** A person whose gender identity is the same as their sex and/or gender assigned at birth.

**Conflate:** To confuse, blend, connect or combine two independent things/ideas.

**Community:** When this book uses the term "community" it refers to a collective group of LGBTQIA+ people and organizations, as well as their supporters, who are all united by common identities, cultures, and/or social goals.

**Demigender:** Someone who has/experiences a partial connection to one or more genders.

**Demisexual/romantic:** A person who only experiences attraction to people with whom they have formed a strong emotional bond.

**DFAB/AFAB/FAAB:** Acronyms for "designated female at birth," "assigned female at birth," and "female assigned at birth."

**Diamoric:** In terms of personal identity, a non-binary person may identify as diamoric to emphasize their own non-binary identity and their attraction to/relationship(s) with other non-binary people. In terms of a relationship, a diamoric relationship or attraction is one that involves at least one non-binary person.

**DMAB/AMAB/MAAB:** Acronyms for "designated male at birth," "assigned male at birth," and "male assigned at birth."

**Enby:** This is a slang term meaning "a non-binary person."

**Erasure:** When an identity is given insufficient representation, made invisible, or its existence is invalidated.

**Female to Female/FTF:** Someone whose sex and/or gender was assigned male at birth and who rejects that their gender was ever male.

**Fluid:** Not fixed, able to change.

**-flexible:** Suffix indicating someone is predominantly attracted to one gender but allows for and acknowledge exceptions. *(Example usages: heteroflexible, homoflexible, etc.)*

**-flux:** In regards to orientation, "flux" is a suffix that indicates that a person's attractions fluctuate in amount or intensity. *(Example usages: biflux, triflux, polyflux, etc.)*

**FTM:** Acronym for "female to male."

**Gay:** This label can refer specifically to men who are attracted to men; it can refer to people who are primary attracted to the same or similar gender as their own; or it can be an umbrella term for anyone who is not straight.

**Gender:** In the context of individual self, gender is the state of being a man, a woman, both, neither, somewhere in between, or something entirely different. In the context of society, gender is a system of classification rooted in social ideas about masculinity and femininity.

**Gender confusion/Gender f\*ck:** A person who deliberately seeks to cause, or enjoys when they create, confusion in regards to their own gender.

**Gender dysphoria:** Distress or unhappiness experienced because one's gender does not match their sex and/or gender assigned at birth.

**Gender euphoria:** Extreme happiness, or comfortability, experienced because a person's gender is being affirmed.

**Gender expression:** The manifestation of one's gender.

**Gender identity:** The identifier (or lack of identifier) someone uses to communicate how they understand their personal gender, navigate within or outside our societal gender systems, and/or desire to be perceived by others.

**Gender indifferent:** Being gender indifferent means being apathetic about one's gender/gender expression.

**Gender neutral:** Having a gender that is neutral.

**Gender nonconforming/Gender diverse/Gender variant/ Gender-expansive:** These are umbrella terms and descriptors which refer to people who identify and/or express themselves in ways that are different from society's binary norms.

**Gender roles:** Societal roles, positions, behaviors, and/or responsibilities allowed or expected from men and women based on societal norms.

**Genderfluid:** Having a gender that changes.

**Genderflux:** Someone whose experience with gender changes (fluctuates) in intensity.

**Genderqueer:** Someone whose gender exists outside of or beyond society's binary concept of gender.

**Graysexual/romantic:** People who experience very low amounts of attraction; people who experience attraction rarely or only under certain conditions; and/or people who are not sure whether they experience attraction.

**Graygender:** This identity involves having a weak sense of gender and/or being somewhat apathetic about one's gender identity/expression.

**Heterosexual/romantic a.k.a. Straight:** Being attracted to the other binary gender.

**Homosexual/romantic:** A person who is attracted to the same or similar gender(s) as their own.

**IAFAB/IAMAB a.k.a. FAFAB/FAMAB:** Acronyms for "intersex assigned female/male at birth" and "forcibly assigned female/male at birth."

**ID:** Shorthand for "identify."

**Intergender:** A person who identifies between or as a mix of the binary genders.

**Internalization:** Conscious or unconscious learning/assimilation of behaviors/attitudes.

**Intersectionality:** The various ways a person or group's combined social identities/roles (e.g. gender, race, socio-economic status, etc.) interact to shape their experience of the world.

**Intersex:** A sex category that includes people whose anatomy does not completely fit into either of society's typical definitions of male or female.

**Lesbian:** Women (as well as non-binary and genderqueer people who feel a connection to womanhood) who are attracted to other women.

**LGBTQIA+:** Stands for lesbian, gay, bisexual, transgender, queer/questioning, intersex, asexual/aromantic, and plus for other identities that are not straight and/or not cisgender.

**Male to Male/MTM:** Someone whose sex and/or gender was assigned female at birth and who rejects that their gender was ever female.

**Man:** Someone who identifies as a man.

**Masexuality/romanticism a.k.a. Androsexuality/ romanticism**: Attraction to men and/or masculinity.

**Maverique:** Someone who has an autonomous gender which exists entirely independent of the binary genders man and woman.

**Maxigender:** Someone who experiences many, and sometimes, all available genders to them.

**Monosexuality/romanticism:** Attraction to a single gender.

**MTF:** Acronym for "male to female."

**Multigender/Polygender:** Someone who has/experiences more than one gender.

**Multisexuality/romanticism a.k.a. Non-monosexuality/ romanticism:** Attractions to more than one gender.

**Neutrois:** Someone whose gender is neutral or null.

**Nomasexual/romantic:** Someone who is attracted to anyone who isn't a man.

**Non-binary/nb:** Existing or identifying outside the sex/gender binary, being neither a man nor woman, or being only partially or a combination of these things.

**Normalize:** to make something accepted as common or natural in society.

**Norms:** Behaviors society has deemed typical or standard and has come to expect.

**Novosexual/romantic:** A person whose attractions change based on the gender(s) they are experiencing.

**Nowomasexual/romantic:** Someone who is attracted to anyone who isn't a woman.

**Pan/Omnigender:** People who experience many, and sometimes, all genders.

**Pansexual/romantic a.k.a. Omnisexual/romantic:** Capable of being attracted to any or all gender(s).

**Policing:** The imposition of norms, or personal beliefs, by way of telling others how they should, or should not, identify, behave, or express themselves. In this book, policing is used in the context of gender and sexuality. *(Example: "You can't do ballet, you're a boy!" or "You can't call yourself a lesbian until you've dated a girl.")*

**Polyamory:** The practice or desire of relationships involving more than two people. Like any relationship, these require communication, honesty, and consent in order to be successful.

**Polysexual/romantic:** Someone who experiences attraction to multiple, but not necessarily all, genders.

**Privilege:** Benefits and opportunities automatically afforded to majorities or non-oppressed groups of people, that are usually unnoticed or taken for granted and occur at the expense of oppressed groups of people.

**Pronouns:** In this book the types of pronouns explored are words used to refer to specific people when their proper names are not being used (e.g. he, she, they, ze, e, etc.). Our society has strong associations between certain pronouns and gender.

**Queer:** An umbrella term or identity taken on by some LGBTQIA+ people to describe a sexual and/or gender identity that falls outside societal norms. This term has a history of being used as a slur. Although it has been reclaimed by many LGBTQIA+ people, not everyone is comfortable using it.

**Questioning:** Being unsure of one's sexual/romantic orientation or gender identity.

**Quoisexual/romantic a.k.a. WTFromantic:** A person who can't tell the difference between attractions they experience, is unsure if they experience attraction, and/or doesn't think romantic and/or sexual attractions are relevant to them.

**Recipsexuality/romanticism:** Experiencing attraction to someone only after knowing that they are attracted to you.

**Same gender loving/SGL:** This term refers to Black LGBTQIA+ people.

**Self-Identification:** The act of identifying a particular way, one that feels right or true for someone.

**Sex:** A socially constructed classification system based on a person's biology. Society typically recognizes only two sex categories, male and female, each with specific biological requirements. The reality though, is that people's biology is often more diverse than society's categories and requirements. Intersex people are an example of this.

**Sex/gender assignment:** Society's propensity to label an infant as male or female, man or woman, at birth, usually based on the appearance of their genitals.

**Skoliosexual/romantic a.k.a. ceterosexual/romantic:** People who are attracted to people of non-binary (nb) genders.

**Society:** The dominant community of people, laws, traditions, values, and culture in a particular area.

**Spectrum:** Concepts and models of identities that challenge mainstream beliefs about the rigidity of sexuality and gender. Spectrums illustrate that people can exist in the spaces between the more commonly established identities.

**-spike:** A suffix that indicates a person's attractions fluctuate. Spike people often feel they experience no attraction, but then suddenly and intensely experience a spike in attraction(s). *(Example usages: acespike, arospike.)*

**Stigma:** Negative associations and/or expectations which are tied to specific groups/labels/identities that are usually based in misconception and/or stereotypes. *(Example: Bisexuals are sometimes stigmatized as being greedy, promiscuous or confused.)*

**Trans man:** Someone who was assigned female at birth and is a man.

**Trans woman:** Someone who was assigned male at birth and is a woman.

**Transfeminine:** A term used to describe someone who was assigned male at birth, and who has a predominantly feminine gender and/or expresses themselves in a way they describe as feminine.

**Transgender/Trans:** An umbrella term for anyone whose gender identity does *not* match their sex and/or gender assigned at birth.

**Transition:** The process of accepting oneself and/or pursuing changes in order to affirm one's gender and/or alleviate dysphoria.

**Transmasculine:** A term used to describe someone who was assigned female at birth, and who has a predominantly masculine gender and/or expresses themselves in a way they describe as masculine.

**Transsexual:** A person whose gender is different from their sex/gender assigned at birth. Sometimes this identity is associated with having undergone and/or wanting to undergo some kind of medical transition. This is an older term that has fallen out of popular usage in favor of the word "transgender."

**Trigender:** Someone who has/experiences three genders.

**Trisexual/romantic:** Someone who experiences attractions to three genders.

**Trysexual/romatic:** Someone who is sexually and/or romantically open to experimenting.

**Umbrella term:** A word or phrase that collectively describes or refers to more than one identity/orientation/group of people. Many of the umbrella terms in this book can also double as specific, or stand-alone identities. *(Example: Genderqueer can be both a specific gender identity as well as an umbrella term which includes many gender nonconforming identities and people.)*

**Validate:** To acknowledge, support, and/or accept that something is real and legitimate.

**Woman:** Someone who identifies as a woman.

**Womasexuality/romanticismm a.k.a. gynesexuality/ romanticism:** Attraction to women and/or femininity.

**Zedsexual/romantic, a.k.a. allosexual/romantic:** A person who experiences sexual/romantic attraction. (A.k.a. someone not on the ace/aro spectrum.)

EXPERIENCE OF SEXUAL ATTRACTION

experiencing _no_ sexual attraction

experiencing _lots_ of sexual attraction

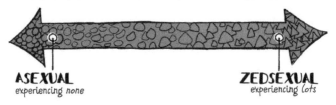

EXPERIENCE OF SEXUAL ATTRACTION

**ASEXUAL**
experiencing _none_

**ZEDSEXUAL**
experiencing _lots_

EXPERIENCE OF SEXUAL ATTRACTION

GRAYSEXUAL

EXPERIENCE OF SEXUAL ATTRACTION

ACEFLUX

# Spectrum

**Words of wisdom from Ash**

"Spectrums are tools or concepts that help us understand identities in complex ways. Oftentimes we see them as visual aids on which we can represent and plot different identities. There are many styles, the most predominant being the linear model. If neither a line, wheel, nor unicorn are your jam though, don't fret! You can always make your own spectral diagram that perfectly represents your sexual, romantic, gender, and any other identity in a totally custom way!"

## EXPERIENCE OF SEXUAL ATTRACTION

A PERSON WHO DOES NOT EXPERIENCE HIGH LEVELS OF SEXUAL ATTRACTION

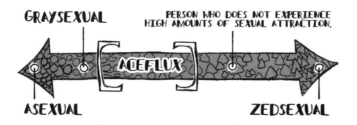

GRAYSEXUAL

PERSON WHO DOES NOT EXPERIENCE HIGH AMOUNTS OF SEXUAL ATTRACTION.

ACEFLUX

ASEXUAL

ZEDSEXUAL

## Where do I feel I am on the gender spectrum today?

_____

_____

_____

_____

_____

_____

_____

_____

_____

_____

_____

_____

_____

_____

_____

_____

_____

_____

_____

_____

_____

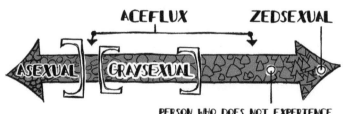

ACEFLUX          ZEDSEXUAL

ASEXUAL   GRAYSEXUAL

PERSON WHO DOES NOT EXPERIENCE
HIGH AMOUNTS OF SEXUAL ATTRACTION.

Draw your own version of the spectrum and see what resonates with you.

# How has my spectrum shifted over the years?

_____

_____

_____

_____

_____

_____

_____

# The Gender Unicorn

Graphic by:
**TSER**
Trans Student Educational Resources

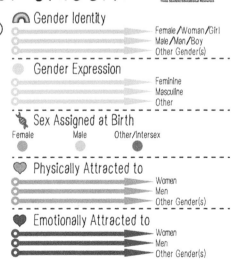

To learn more, go to:
www.transstudent.org/gender

Design by Landyn Pan and Anna Moore

### Gender Identity
- Female/Woman/Girl
- Male/Man/Boy
- Other Gender(s)

### Gender Expression
- Feminine
- Masculine
- Other

### Sex Assigned at Birth
Female    Male    Other/Intersex

### Physically Attracted to
- Women
- Men
- Other Gender(s)

### Emotionally Attracted to
- Women
- Men
- Other Gender(s)

# Gender

## Words of wisdom from Ash

"Learning that one's biology is different than they expected can be a surreal, confusing experience. No matter what you think the correct way to view sex is, it's undeniable that there is more than just male and female. When it comes to sex, our bodies are complex and beautifully diverse. This is why sex is most definitely not a binary thing."

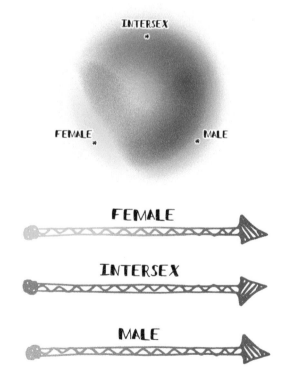

INTERSEX

FEMALE          MALE

FEMALE

INTERSEX

MALE

# What does (biological) sex mean to me?

# What does gender mean to me?

Try creating a gender collage and reflect on the images you choose to include.

# GENDER IS:

# Identity

**Words of wisdom from Ash**

"It is fine if you find yourself lost or confused at all while perusing a detailed list of terms. I want to offer a word of encouragement: You are doing good just by being curious and open to different identities."

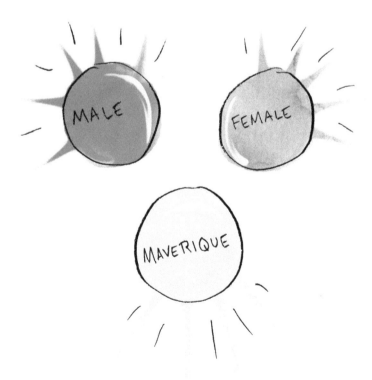

**Do I feel trapped inside my body or does it fit just right? Or am I somewhere in between?**

# What do I love about my body?

## What fears do I think someone who is considering transitioning feels?

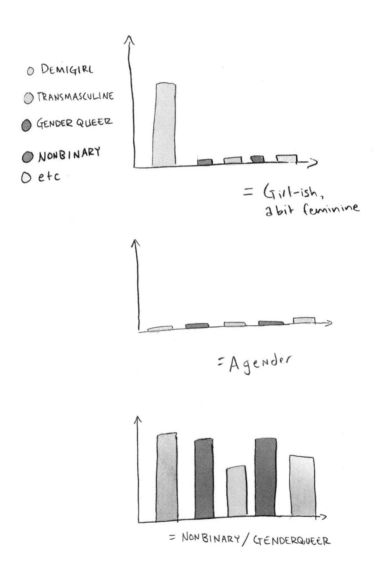

○ DEMIGIRL

◑ TRANSMASCULINE

● GENDER QUEER

● NONBINARY

○ etc

= Girl-ish, a bit feminine

= Agender

= NONBINARY / GENDERQUEER

# Sexuality and Romance

### Words of wisdom from Ash

"If you determine that you do feel sexual attraction, you should know this experience is not uniform or identical for everyone. Different people's sexual attractions are highly diverse. One of the most obvious examples of this is gender preference."

# How do you feel about kissing?

# How do you feel about hugging or snuggling?

**What role does physical intimacy play in my relationships? What role do I want it to play?**

# Learn more about LGBTQ+ history and the community.

ISBN 9781633534094
PRICE $16.95
TRIM 5.5x8.25

Mango Publishing, established in 2014, publishes an eclectic list of books by diverse authors—both new and established voices—on topics ranging from business, personal growth, women's empowerment, LGBTQ studies, health, and spirituality to history, popular culture, time management, decluttering, lifestyle, mental wellness, aging, and sustainable living. We were recently named 2019 *and* 2020's #1 fastest-growing independent publisher by *Publishers Weekly.* Our success is driven by our main goal, which is to publish high-quality books that will entertain readers as well as make a positive difference in their lives.

Our readers are our most important resource; we value your input, suggestions, and ideas. We'd love to hear from you— after all, we are publishing books for you!

Please stay in touch with us and follow us at:

Facebook: Mango Publishing
Twitter: @MangoPublishing
Instagram: @MangoPublishing
LinkedIn: Mango Publishing
Pinterest: Mango Publishing
Newsletter: mangopublishinggroup.com/newsletter

Join us on Mango's journey to reinvent publishing, one book at a time.

CPSIA information can be obtained
at www.ICGtesting.com
Printed in the USA
JSHW010746110322
23800JS00008B/34

9 781642 509472